BOOKWORMS

Animal Homes

A Lion's Den

Arthur Best

Cavendish Square
New York

Published in 2019 by Cavendish Square Publishing, LLC
243 5th Avenue, Suite 136, New York, NY 10016

First Edition

Website: cavendishsq.com

Library of Congress Cataloging-in-Publication Data

Names: Best, B. J., 1976- , author.
Title: A Lion's Den / Arthur Best.
Description: New York : Cavendish Square, 2018. | Series: Animal homes |
Includes index. | Audience: Grades K to 2. |
Identifiers: LCCN 2017052043 (print) | LCCN 2017053938 (ebook) | ISBN
9781502636638 (ebook) | ISBN 9781502636621 (library bound) | ISBN
9781502636645 (pbk.) | ISBN 9781502636652 (6 pack)
Subjects: LCSH: Lion--Juvenile literature.
Classification: LCC QL737.C23 (ebook) | LCC QL737.C23 B475 2018 (print) | DDC 599.75/5--dc23
LC record available at https://lccn.loc.gov/2017052043

Editorial Director: David McNamara
Copy Editor: Rebecca Rohan
Associate Art Director: Amy Greenan
Designer: Megan Metté
Production Coordinator: Karol Szymczuk
Photo Research: J8 Media

The photographs in this book are used by permission and through the courtesy of: Cover Dominique Del9no/Biosphoto/Getty Images; p. 5 Michael Potter11/Shutterstock.com; p. 7 East Village Images/Shutterstock.com; p. 9 Maggy Meyer/Shutterstock.com; p. 11 MaryU/Shutterstock.com; p. 13 Stefonlinton/iStock/Thinkstock; p. 15 Litoshenko Oleksii/Shutterstock.com; p. 17 ©iStockphoto.com/GP232; p. 19 JJMaree/iStock/Thinkstock; p. 21 Jonathan & Angela Scott/AWL Images/Getty Images.

Printed in the United States of America

Contents

Lions are big.

They are cats.

They roar.

Lions live in **Africa**.

They live in grass.

There are not many trees.

Lions live in groups.

The groups are called **prides**.

The prides move.

The lions walk.

Their home is the grass.

They sleep there.

Lions have babies.

The babies are called **cubs**.

The mother finds a home.

The cubs live there.

The home is called a **den**.

The den is made of **bushes**.

It is safe.

The cubs can hide.

The cubs grow.

The mother feeds them.

The cubs get older.

They leave the den.

They join the pride!

New Words

Africa (AF-rih-kuh) One of Earth's seven huge pieces of land.

bushes (BUSH-ez) Small trees.

cubs (CUBZ) Baby lions.

den (DEN) A cub's home.

prides (PRYDZ) Groups of lions.

Index

About the Author

Arthur Best lives in Wisconsin with his wife and son. He has written many other books for children. He has seen a lion in Africa.

About BOOKWORMS

Bookworms help independent readers gain reading confidence through high-frequency words, simple sentences, and strong picture/text support. Each book explores a concept that helps children relate what they read to the world they live in.